MW00779347

HOW TO

CHANGE YOUR SPIRITUAL LIFE IN 40 DAYS

Heart Ink Press
LLC

· BISHOP JOEL BROWN

HOW TO

CHANGE YOUR
SPIRITUAL LIFE IN
40 DAYS

BISHOP JOEL BROWN

Copyright © 2020 by Joseph W. Brown II

All rights reserved. This book is protected under the copyright laws of the United States of America. This book may not be copied or reprinted for commercial gain or profit. The use of short quotations or occasional page copying for personal or group study is permitted and encouraged. Permission will be granted upon request. Unless otherwise identified, scripture quotations are from the King James Version of the Bible. Other versions will be followed by their abbreviation. For example, a scripture quoted from the New King James Version will be followed by NKJV. All emphasis, revelation, interpretation, and understanding are that of the Author.

Take note that Jesus, Christ, Lord and God are referred to as "He" as well as "he" in this book. This purpose is to make sure no one gets confused with ownership and point of subject in particular areas of the book.

ISBN: 978-0-9835854-9-7

Heart.Ink Press, LLC "Manifesting

Dreams and Visions...
... Tuned to the Beat of Your Heart"

CONTENTS

INTRODUCTION

As a Pastor, Attorney and Professor I have the pleasure and privilege of meeting with men and women and counseling them regarding life and spiritual matters. What I have come to learn is that many people believe that they love God and say that they love God, but their actions (not following the Word, not going to church, etc.) show that they're half in and half out of the things of God. Realizing this truth, a need for deliverance was necessary for them. From my meetings with different individuals, I have found that most people are not aware of some of the very practical steps that they can take in order to see change and deliverance in their lives. Because of this, a seed was planted for How to Change Your Spiritual Life in 40 Days. Get ready because embarking on this journey will produce a major life change!

For 40 days, I challenge you to read at least 2 chapters of the Bible (1 Old Testament chapter and 1 New Testament chapter) every single day. I challenge you to listen to at least one message of the Word of God once a day. I challenge you to do at least 5 minutes of declarations everyday (specific). I challenge you to be in church whenever it is in session. I challenge you to not listen to secular music.

INTRODUCTION

I challenge you to not watch any rated R movies. I challenge you to not watch any rated TV-MA shows or movies. I challenge you to not look at anything inappropriate, including porn. I challenge you to not masturbate. I challenge you to not curse. I challenge you to not gossip. I challenge you to invite someone to church. I challenge you to tithe. I challenge you to fast from all meats and all sweets. I challenge you to take a break and not use any social media (Facebook, Instagram, Snap Chat, etc.) except for ministry and/or business purposes. I challenge you to have an accountability partner that will check on your progress every day or every other day. As you adhere to these challenges, watch God move in your life in ways you have never seen!

With this 40-day challenge, I encourage you to get a mentor or at the very least an accountability partner that will hold you accountable each and every day. Some days will be super easy. Other days, it will be a press and you will want to give up. That is why you need someone in your corner every day for 40 days encouraging you to complete the challenge and see it through. And when you follow these principles outlined in the next few chapters, your very HEART will change, your very DESIRES will change, your very LIFE will change!

1

PREPARING FOR ACTION

We have all been created in the image of divinity, but because of sin there is a perversion in each of us. No one can escape this unless they are covered by the blood of Jesus. However, just because you have eternal salvation it does not mean that your mind is right. We must constantly renew our minds to conform to the image of God (see Romans 12:2). Hearing a preacher once a week is not enough. You must listen to a message of faith daily (see Romans 10:17). You must read the Word of God daily (see Joshua 1:8).

In the natural, I usually eat at least three times a day; breakfast, lunch and dinner (and snacks, to be honest!). If I skip breakfast, I am usually pretty hungry by lunch.

> *We must constantly renew our minds to conform to the image of God.*

If I skip breakfast and lunch, I am very hungry by dinner. And if I do not eat that day for whatever reason, I can be ravenous the next day! But what if I don't eat that next day? I start to lose strength. And then how about the next day? And then the next day? What if I go 6 full days without eating? And then after the 6 full days of not eating anything, I eat one meal on Sunday, and then repeat that again? And then on vacations I sometimes skip the Sunday meal as well? I would barely be able to function! I would constantly be tired, my immune system would be down, and I would barely be able to get any work done.

Well, that's how too many people live their lives. They only feed their spirit man once a week (if that) and they are constantly spiritually weary. Their spiritual immune system is down, so they are more susceptible to the attacks of the enemy, and they are barely able to get any ministry work done. Just as we feed our natural man, we must feed our spirit man. But what are you feeding your spirit? Our minds are like minicomputers, constantly being programmed and updated. Your mind is going to receive and process either trash or Godliness. What are you downloading into your system?

In these next 40 days, you will change your operating system through the 40-day challenge.

2

CHANGING OUR MINDS

Human beings are tripartite beings. Tripartite is a very fancy theological term meaning that we are made up of spirit, soul and body. Our spirit is the eternal part of our being that communes with God. Our soul is the seat of our emotions, our thoughts, our memories, etc. Our body is the physical shell that houses our spirit and soul. This is very important to remember because many people live as if there is only the physical. But in reality, we are just a spiritual being having an earthly encounter! If it is important to maintain our physical bodies for our brief sojourn on this planet Earth, how much more important is it to maintain our spirit for our eternal journey once our time on this earth is over? One of the places to begin with answering this question is within our soul, within the seat of our emotions, our heart and mind.

It is important to change our minds because man was born into sin, into the kingdom of darkness. However, once we are saved, the Bible says that the Lord has "translated us into the kingdom of his dear Son" (Colossians 1:13). We are coming from a system, a worldview, an ideology, a mindset of darkness to the kingdom of light. Now that we are in the kingdom of light, we have to put away our old mindsets (our old way of thinking) and think like God thinks.

Isaiah 55:8-9 (KJV)

"For my thoughts are not your thoughts, neither are your ways my ways, saith the LORD. For as the heavens are higher than the earth, so are my ways higher than your ways, and my thoughts than your thoughts."

When we come into the kingdom of light, we have access to God's thoughts and God's ways. But many times, we try to bring God's thoughts down to our way of thinking as opposed to elevating our thoughts to God's way of thinking. Is this because we don't know how to elevate our thoughts?

Joshua 1:8 states, "This book of the law shall not depart out of thy mouth; but thou shalt meditate therein day and night, that thou mayest observe to do according to all that is written

> *When we come into the kingdom of light, we have access to God's thoughts and God's ways.*

therein: for then thou shalt make thy way prosperous, and then thou shalt have good success." While I was reading and meditating on Joshua 1:8, the Lord put a formula on my heart. It simply is:

> **SPEAK** the word
> +
> **MEDITATE** on the word
> +
> **ACT** on the word
>
> = Prosperity and Good Success!!!

CHANGING OUR MINDS

If we are speaking the Word daily, if we are meditating on the Word daily, and if we are acting on the Word daily, we will have prosperity and good success! This is how we bring our thoughts up to God-s thoughts and our ways up to God-s ways! It's very simple in its approach, if not in execution.

I have found that one of the keys to growing spiritually is to integrate this formula into your daily life. The Word of God is special. It is not just another book. The Word is God embodied in flesh as a propitiation for our sins (cf. John 1:14 and 1 John 2:2)! And for the believer, there is a supernatural occurrence that happens every time we read the Word! It is "...life unto those that find them, and health to all their flesh" (Proverbs 4:22, KJV). The Word is an illumination to our paths. It is doctrine, it is exhortation. It is the source of faith, it is unchangeable. It is either true, and your guide or it has some truth but is otherwise an ancient doctrine. You have to decide the last one for yourself.

Some people may say, "well, if the Word was true, then why don't I have..." (fill in the blank)? Do you know how many times I have thought or asked that over the years? What I have learned is that it is never the Word of God that is lacking or debatable. It is ALWAYS our response, or lack of response, to the Word that causes its operation or lack of operation in our lives. Let God be true, and every man be a liar! Instead of questioning the validity and veracity of the scriptures, if we have not seen a promise of God take place yet in our life, we should ALWAYS start with a self-examination.

> *The Word is an illumination to our paths. It is doctrine, it is exhortation. It is the source of faith, it is unchangeable.*

"Lord, I know that your Word is true, and I believe you. Please reveal to me what I am doing or what I am not doing that may be hindering the promises of your Word from being a present reality in my life." As we begin to live our lives, knowing God to be true, we realize that it is never the Word of God that is lacking, but rather something lacking in us. With this new perspective, we can then approach the promises of God with the correct attitude, outlook and position of faith; taking ahold of every promise of God for our lives and believing and receiving that it is ours!

3

SPEAKING THE WORD OF GOD

T he Bible is very clear on the importance of our speech. As a
matter of fact, the Word tells us in Genesis that God said (9
times in the first chapter) for the heavens and earth to come into effect.
James tells us that "Indeed, we all make many mistakes. For if we could
control our tongues, we would be perfect and could also control
ourselves in every other way" (James 3:2, NLT). There is a great
importance attached to what we say.

Proverbs 18:21a (KJV) states, "Death and life are in the power of the
tongue." Job 22:28 (KJV) says, "Thou shalt also decree a thing, and it
shall be established unto thee." Jesus says in Mark 11:23 (KJV), "For
verily I say unto you, That whosoever **shall say** unto this mountain, Be
thou removed, and be thou cast into the sea; and shall not doubt in his
heart, but shall believe that those things **which he saith** shall come to
pass; he shall have **whatsoever he saith**." There are many more
examples in scriptures that describe the importance and power of the
tongue, but the final one I will mention here is a return back to our
formula:

Joshua 1:8 (KJV), "This book of the law shall not depart **out of thy
mouth**."

SPEAKING THE WORD OF GOD

There are many people who decry making declarations based upon it being a "new age" doctrine. That is outright false! The Word of God has numerous examples of the power of the tongue; of the power of saying life as opposed to death, and of being very careful in our speech! The church did not get positive confession from the world, the world got it from the church! A law is a law whether you recognize it as a law or not. The law is working whether you realize it or not! Continue to say your words do not matter and speak frivolously in your life and watch how your life lines up with what you are saying! Change your words and change your life!

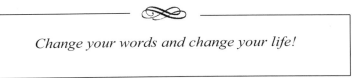

Change your words and change your life!

DON'T ABORT YOUR BABY

We are all pregnant with potential. Everyone has a God designed assignment that they were placed on this earth to accomplish. Make sure that your words always line up with what God is trying to birth through you.

Mary, the mother of Jesus, was a young virgin when the angel of the Lord came to her and informed her that she would give birth to our Lord and Savior, Jesus Christ. She asked the angel, "How can this be, seeing I know not a man?" (Luke 1:34, KJV). Mary wanted to know the mechanics because she was a virgin. Once the angel told her how (verses 35-37), Mary responded, "be it unto me according to thy word" (verse 38).

SPEAKING THE WORD OF GOD

Even though it was impossible, she believed that God could do it! Even though your destiny, assignment, calling or purpose may seem impossible, if it is God-given, our response should be like Mary's; well Lord, be it unto me! Mary was careful not to say anything that would abort her destiny. Her cousin's husband, Zacharias, was a different story altogether.

When the angel of the Lord came to the man of God, the priest Zacharias, and told him about the miraculous pregnancy and birth that was about to take place with his wife, his response was not one of faith. Zacharias asks, "Whereby shall I know this? for I am an old man, and my wife well stricken in years" (Luke 1:18). Zacharias' statement is dripping with unbelief. The angel of the Lord immediately recognized this and before Zacharias could utter more words of unbelief or make statements that could potentially abort destiny, Gabriel, the angel, preserved the birth by causing Zacharias not to be able to speak (Luke 1:19-22). John the Baptist's (Zacharias' son) mission was too important to be stopped even before it began by words of doubt. Some people today are aborting their God given destinies because they are speaking words full of doubt and fear.

Stop trying to birth destiny in the natural! How are you going to birth supernatural purpose and destiny by saying the same negative things you have been repeating over the years? How are you going to birth supernatural purpose and destiny with natural means? If God has put an assignment on your heart bigger than what you can do in the natural, why are you still trying to use the natural to figure out how it is going to work?

> *Stop trying to birth destiny in the natural!*

SPEAKING THE WORD OF GOD

Give voice to the Word of God by faith! Don't stop, hinder or prolong the manifestation of the blessing of God in your life by not being able to tame your tongue. Watch your tongue, don't abort your destiny through negative declarations or by talking about people!

4

MEDITATING ON THE WORD OF GOD

A s you meditate on the Word of God, God is able to reveal Himself to you. He is able to give you a revelation of how He thinks, moves and acts. When we meditate on the Word of God, we can receive revelation of the will of God.

Meditating on the Word of God causes
our minds to process the right things.

It causes us to change our mindsets, our world views, and our beliefs. When you have right beliefs, you get right actions and right words. When you have right actions and right words, you get right results. When you have wrong beliefs, you get wrong actions and wrong words. When you have wrong actions or wrong words, you get wrong results.

Luke 6:45 (NLT) states, "A good person produces good things from the treasury of a good heart, and an evil person produces evil things from the treasury of an evil heart. What you say flows from what is in your heart." And Proverbs 4:23 emphasizes that your thoughts matter, "Above all else, guard your heart, for everything you do flows from it."

MEDITATING ON THE WORD OF GOD

How do you guard your heart? You guard your heart (or your mind, will and emotions) by watching what goes into it. Remember! Your mind is like a computer processor – if you put in the proper programming, you get the desired results. But if you put trash in, you will eventually get trash coming out. It is very important to watch what kind of things you are listening to, what kind of things you are watching, and what kind of conversations you are having. It may not be a sin to watch a certain type of movie, but that movie may be filling you with trash. It may not be a sin to listen to a certain type of music, but that music may be filling your mind with trash. Over the next 40 days, there are some things specifically that I am requesting that you refrain from (rated R movies, social media, etc.) to ensure that you are doing your job to keep trash out of your system.

CHANGE THE WAY YOU THINK

When you begin to dwell in the Word of God, the first thing you discover is that the Word goes absolutely contrary to the way you're accustomed to thinking. To the world, thinking like the Bible exhorts us to think may even seem like foolishness! You must understand that this battle that you are fighting is about your mind. This battle is not about your marriage, it's not about your family, it's not about your relationships, it's not about your future, it's not about your destiny, and it's not about your money. This battle is about your mind! I don't care WHAT you are going through, if you align your mind with the Word of God, then you can make it! And I don't care how frivolous the battle may seem; if your mind isn't right, it can send you into a depression! You win or lose the battle in your mind before any place else.

MEDITATING ON THE WORD OF GOD

> *This battle is about your mind! I don't care*
> *WHAT you are going through, if you align*
> *your mind with the Word of God,* **then you**
> **can make it!**

Daily renew your mind by meditating and listening to the Word of God every single day. Romans 12:2 (NLT) states, "Don't copy the behavior and customs of this world, but let God transform you into a new person by changing the way you think. Then you will learn to know God's will for you, which is good and pleasing and perfect."

Make up your mind that you will change your way of thinking. You will focus on the good, not the bad. You will believe God's Word, and not a negative report that goes contrary to God's Word. You will change the way you think about your marriage, you will change the way you think about your health, and you will change the way you think about your life! Over these 40 days, refocus your mind on who you are as a Christian and who you serve. God is beyond us. God is the King of the universe. God is the Great I AM! We serve a supernatural God who does supernatural things, through a supernatural people! No longer discount the supernatural from taking place in your life. The God whom we serve is the same God who created the heavens and the earth. The God whom we serve is the same God who parted the Red Sea. The God that we serve is the same God that raised Jesus from the dead! Stop relegating God to a natural being that you can fully comprehend!

Change the way you think about God! Change the way you think about church! Change the way you think about being a Christian!

5

ACTING OR DOING THE WORD OF GOD

Now that we are speaking the right words and meditating on the Word of God day and night, we can take the next step of doing the Word so that we can prosper and have good success. Jesus said that we would do "greater works" if we believe on Him (John 14:12). We are called to do greater works to further expand the kingdom of God, to destroy the works of the enemy and to bring glory to God.

As we seek to act on the Word of God, we can take the example of Jesus of only doing what He saw the Father do (John 5:19) and by only saying what He heard the Father say (John 12:49). As we speak and meditate on the Word of God consistently, God will give us what to do in regard to the Word of God to see the manifestation of His promises in our life. During the next 40 days, God may begin to show you a problem or issue that is hindering the manifestation of His promises in your life.

*As we speak and meditate on the Word of God consistently, **God will give us what to do** in regard to the Word of God to see the manifestation of His promises in our life.*

ACTING OR DOING THE WORD OF GOD

Thankfully, there IS a solution to your problem or issue! God has a customized solution to every problem or issue you may face in this life. Over these next 40 days, make a request known, "Lord, please give me what to say and what to do for my customized solution to my problem or issue."

The Word of God is filled with examples of God giving individuals what to say or what to do in order to see prosperity and good success in their lives. He told Joshua to walk around the wall of Jericho one time for six days and then seven times on

God has a customized solution to every problem or issue you may face in this life.

the seventh day and to blow the trumpets (see Joshua 6:1-5). He told Naaman through Elisha the prophet to wash in the dirty Jordan River (see 2 Kings 5:10). He told the lame man through Peter and John to rise up and walk (see Acts 3:1-6).

WATCH OUT FOR SAUL'S ARMOR

We need to be careful by only allowing God to give us what to say and what to do. When we look at the account of David and Goliath, we see where a man with a God given assignment almost subjected himself to man's wisdom. In 1 Samuel 17:8-9, we get a chance to see just how high the stakes were in this battle against Goliath. If the champion of Israel wins, the Philistines become the subjects of the Israelites. If Goliath wins, then the Israelites become the subjects of the Philistines. When David hears about this, he tells Saul that he will fight on behalf of Israel. At first Saul referenced David's youth and inexperience, but he eventually acquiesced to the call of God on David's life and allowed him to be the champion for Israel (1 Samuel 17:32-37).

ACTING OR DOING THE WORD OF GOD

Even though Saul had a moment of spiritual clarity and agreed with David, Saul's thinking reverted to his old way of thinking; an unrenewed mindset. Saul offered David his own tunic, and he put a coat of armor on David and a bronze helmet on his head (verse 38).

David even tried on a sword, but ultimately took all of them off to take his own staff, sling and five smooth stones (verses 39-40).

We must always be cautious to only do what God says to do and to only say what God says to say.

When God gives you an assignment, seek the counsel of God and Godly spiritual advisors. Otherwise, people

> *Watch out for natural wisdom to conduct a* ***God assignment.***

will acquiesce to your God given assignment but will try to direct you, from the natural, in the way they think is best for you to carry out your God given assignment. This will cause you to lose the battle. So, watch out for Saul's armor. Watch out for natural wisdom to conduct a God assignment.

In reading the Word of God, listen in your spirit for a customized word from the Lord to help you carry out your assignment or a solution to your issue. Let's believe God and pray this prayer over the next 40 days, "Lord, please give me a customized word to act upon for my situation. In Jesus' name, Amen."

Prayer:
Lord, please give me a customized word to act upon for my situation. In Jesus' name, Amen.

6

HOW TO READ THE ROADMAP

As you get started on your 40-day journey I have provided a roadmap to keep you headed in the direction of spiritual growth. What I have laid out in the roadmap is by no means comprehensive, but it is to be considered the very minimum that you do every day for the next 40 days. This isn't some magic bullet or get rich quick scheme. To follow this roadmap, it will take **work, discipline, and consistency**. But if you can make it through, I guarantee you that your life will never be the same again!

PRAYING THE WORD

Whenever we pray, we should always find a scriptural basis for our prayers.

> *God is not bound to do whatever we say. But the Lord God Almighty is bound to what He has said, which is contained in His Word.*

The effective prayer is praying the Word. Sometimes people may ask, "How exactly do I pray the scriptures?"

HOW TO READ THE ROADMAP

Simply put, insert your name into them. For example,

Romans 4:5 (NLT) states:
"But people are counted as righteous, not because of their work, but because of their faith in God who forgives sinners."

First, read the scripture out Lord (I believe it is powerful to hear the Word of God expressed through your voice), and then declare/pray that "*I am* counted as righteous, not because of *my* work, but because of *my* faith in God who forgives sinners,"

1 Corinthians 13:13 (NLT) states:
"Three things will last forever—faith, hope, and love—and the greatest of these is love."

I have faith, hope, and love and the greatest *in me* is love.

Proverbs 3:5-6 (KJV) states:
"Trust in the Lord with all thine heart; and lean not unto thine own understanding. In all thy ways acknowledge him, and he shall direct thy paths."

I trust in you Lord with all *of my* heart; and *I am* not leaning to *my* own understanding. In all of *my* ways *I am* acknowledging you Lord, and you Lord are directing *my* paths.

Whenever we pray, we should strive to use
*scriptures or have a **scriptural basis** for*
our prayers.

If you are going through a particular situation and you don't know what scripture or scripture reference to use for your prayers, then Google it. Type a few terms in the search bar and include "prayers for (insert your prayer topic)" and then get some scriptures that you can stand on in prayer and believe God for a change in your situation. I have provided some scriptures on your roadmap that you can pray during these 40 days, but please, by no means feel restricted to just these.

DECLARATIONS

I have previously written about the importance of what you say. We must use our tongues offensively and defensively. We must use our tongues to declare the truth of God in our lives, and we must guard our tongues against speaking negative, evil and hurtful things to ourselves and to others. For the next 40 days (and prayerfully for the rest of your life), you will declare things over your life based on the scriptures; based on what is found in the Word of God. Some of the declarations you will find on your roadmap, I will present here:

- Thank you, Lord, that this is a great day!

- I plead the blood of Jesus over my life on today!

- The manifested presence and power of God is in my home, is in my family, is in my church and is in everything that I do!

- Life is so sweet with the Lord!

- I am blessed and cannot be cursed!

- Thank you, Lord, for directing my steps and I know that something great is going to happen to me today!

- Seeds of discouragement will never take root in my grateful heart!

- I do not have a care in this world because I've cast every one of them onto my Lord!

❧ I will stay in peace on today. Nothing will move me!

❧ I forgive everyone who has done me wrong. I don't hold anything against anyone!

LISTENING TO THE WORD

The Bible speaks a lot about faith. *The just shall live by faith (Romans 1:17). We walk by faith and not by sight (2 Corinthians 5:7). Without faith it is impossible to please God (Hebrews 11:6).*

> *Because faith is so important, it becomes essential for us to find out how we can **build our faith.***

Throughout the Bible, the only place where I have found where faith can be increased (the disciples actually asked the Lord to increase their faith, but it was a request, not an affirmation that it would be done; see Luke 17:5) is in Romans.

Romans 10:13-17 (KJV)
For whosoever shall call upon the name of the Lord shall be saved. How then shall they call on him in whom they have not believed? and how shall they believe in him of whom they have not heard? and how shall they hear without a preacher?

And how shall they preach, except they be sent? as it is written, How beautiful are the feet of them that preach the gospel of peace, and bring glad tidings of good things! But they have not all obeyed the gospel. For Esaias saith, Lord, who hath believed our report? So then faith cometh by hearing, and hearing by the word of God.

You have to hear the word of God in order for faith to come (Romans 10:17)! And faith does come when you hear the Word of God from a sent preacher (Romans 10:15). What or who is a sent preacher? A sent preacher is sent from God to minister the word of God so that faith can come. You can be your own sent preacher, and others that the Lord reveals to you. But every preacher that preaches is not sent, so therefore, every preacher that you hear is not producing faith in you.

As a matter of fact, some preachers impart more fear than faith, intellectualism than revelation, or soulish excitement rather than spiritual stimulation.

Faith is needed to get through these 40 days, and that is why the requirement of hearing the word of God proclaimed through a sent preacher is so vital.

If you hear something that you are unsure of, first check it by the Word of God. If it is not scriptural, then throw it away. If it is scriptural, then don't just reject it, but ask the Lord to help you to understand it to receive the revelation of it.

GOING TO CHURCH

Another important aspect of the 40-day challenge is being in church whenever possible. Online church does not qualify. There is something powerful about community. There is something sacred about being around the people of God continually. And there is biblical precedent to come to the house of the Lord.

The early church devoted themselves to four things: the apostles' teaching, to fellowship, to sharing in meals and to prayer (Acts 2:42). Church has a spiritual component and a social component. The spiritual component encompasses, but is not limited to, that of worshipping and praising God, using your spiritual gifts, and learning the statutes of God. The social component encompasses, but is not limited to, encouragement, community, and fellowship. The Psalms speak of praising God corporately (Psalm 107:32) and being happy about going to God's house (Psalm 122:1). Hebrews speaks of the people of God not forsaking gathering together corporately, although some are failing to do so (Hebrews 10:25).

THE ROADMAP

For 40 days, I challenge you to read at least 2 chapters of the Bible (1 Old Testament chapter and 1 New Testament chapter) every single day. I challenge you to listen to at least one message of the Word of God once a day. I challenge you to do at least 5 minutes of declarations everyday (specific). I challenge you to be in church whenever it is in session. I challenge you to not listen to secular music. I challenge you to not watch any rated R movies. I challenge you to not watch any rated TV-MA shows or movies. I challenge you to not look at anything inappropriate, including porn. I challenge you to not masturbate. I challenge you to not curse. I challenge you to not gossip. I challenge you to invite someone to church. I challenge you to tithe. I challenge you to fast from all meats and all sweets. I challenge you to take a break and not use any social media (Facebook, Instagram, Snap chat, etc.) except for ministry and/or business purposes. I challenge you to have an accountability partner that will check on your progress every day or every other day. As you adhere to these challenges, watch God move in your life in ways you have never seen!

In general, all of this takes around an hour to an hour and 15 minutes daily

Read one chapter in the Bible every day:

Start each reading with this prayer, "Most Holy, Awesome and Gracious Lord, please forgive me if I have done anything that is not pleasing in your sight. Lord Jesus, please open up my mind to understand the scriptures and please give me the Spirit of wisdom and revelation in the knowledge of you and let the eyes of my understanding be enlightened. In Jesus' name I pray, Amen."

The book of James is an excellent book to start with. Then let the Lord lead you or go to Matthew and continue through the New Testament. I find it to be very beneficial to read the Word of God **out loud**.

Read these scriptures daily, then pray them by putting yourself (I, me, my, etc.) into the scriptures.

Mark 11:22-25 (KJV)

"And Jesus answering saith unto them, Have faith in God. For verily I say unto you, That whosoever shall say unto this mountain, Be thou removed, and be thou cast into the sea; and shall not doubt in his heart, but shall believe that those things which he saith shall come to pass; he shall have whatsoever he saith. Therefore I say unto you, What things soever ye desire, when ye pray, believe that ye receive them, and ye shall have them. And when ye stand praying, forgive, if ye have ought against any: that your Father also which is in heaven may forgive you your trespasses."

Romans 4:5 (NLT)

"But people are counted as righteous, not because of their work, but because of their faith in God who forgives sinners."

Proverbs 3:5-6 (KJV)

"Trust in the Lord with all thine heart; and lean not unto thine own understanding. In all thy ways acknowledge him, and he shall direct thy paths."

I Peter 5:7 (KJV)

"Casting all your care upon him; for he careth for you."

Matthew 11:28-30 (KJV)

"Come unto me, all ye that labour and are heavy laden, and I will give you rest. Take my yoke upon you, and learn of me; for I am meek and lowly in heart: and ye shall find rest unto your souls. For my yoke is easy, and my burden is light."

Philippians 4:19 (KJV)

"But my God shall supply all your need according to his riches in glory by Christ Jesus."

Proverbs 4:23 (KJV)

"Keep thy heart with all diligence; for out of it are the issues of life."

James 1:5 (NIV)

"If any of you lacks wisdom, he should ask God, who gives generously to all without finding fault, and it will be given to him."

1 Peter 3:10-11 (NLT)

"For the Scriptures say, 'If you want to enjoy life and see many happy days, keep your tongue from speaking evil and your lips from telling lies. Turn away from evil and do good. Search for peace, and work to maintain it.'"

Psalm 19:14 (KJV)

"Let the words of my mouth and the meditation of my heart be acceptable in Thy sight, O Lord, my Strength and my Redeemer."

Psalms 34:1 (KJV)

"I will bless the LORD at all times: His praise shall continually be in my mouth."

Psalms 131:1 (NLT)

"LORD, my heart is not proud; my eyes are not haughty. I don't concern myself with matters too great or too awesome for me to grasp."

I Timothy 1:7 (KJV)

"For God hath not given us the spirit of fear; but of power, and of love, and of a sound mind."

Psalms 101:3-4 (ESV)

"I will not set before my eyes anything that is worthless. I hate the work of those who fall away; it shall not cling to me. A perverse heart shall be far from me; I will know nothing of evil."

Galatians 5:22-23 (NLT)

"But the Holy Spirit produces this kind of fruit in our lives: love, joy, peace, patience, kindness, goodness, faithfulness, gentleness, and self-control. There is no law against these things!"

DECLARE (SAY) THESE DAILY:

- Father God, in the name of Jesus,

- Thank you, Lord, that this is a great day!

- I plead the blood of Jesus over my life on today!

- The manifested presence and power of God is in my home, is in my family, is in my church and is in everything that I do!

- Let the aroma of heaven surround me! Life

- is so sweet with the Lord!

- I am blessed and cannot be cursed! I am the head and not the tail!

- I am above only and not beneath! I am a lender and not a borrower!

- I am blessed, happy, healthy, whole, and secure!

- Thank you, Lord, for directing my steps and I know that something great is going to happen to me today!

- Seeds of discouragement will never take root in my grateful heart! I

- will not complain!

- I will always stay grateful!

- I believe that all my needs are met!

- I call all of my bills paid in Jesus' name!

- I do not have a care in this world because I've cast every one of them onto my Lord!

- I will stay in peace on today. Nothing will move me!

- I forgive everyone who has done me wrong. I don't hold anything against anyone!

- I am anointed to operate on a level that the world is not familiar with all for the glory of God!

- I am anointed to do ministry on a level that the world is not familiar with all for the glory of God!

- I am anointed to do ministry on a level that the American church is not familiar with all for the glory of God!

- I am a person of destiny!

- I am equipped!

- I am talented, I am creative, and I am strong! I am brilliant! I

- am disciplined!

- I am anointed! I

- am healed!

- Thank you, Lord, that I have been redeemed!

- Thank you, Lord, that I never have sickness or disease!

- I am faithful, always responsible, and completely trustworthy!

- I take good care of my body. I eat right, I look good, I feel good, and I weigh what God wants me to weigh!

- Pain cannot successfully come against my body because Jesus bore all my pain!

- I am whole! I

- am secure!

- I am made righteous with God through my faith in Jesus!

- I am receiving divine parables and Godly examples to illustrate and illuminate the Word of God that I speak!

- God is taking our ministry where no ministry has ever gone!

- The presence of God on this Sunday will be the heaviest it has ever been at my church!

- I was designed for a purpose!

- I am handsome (or I am beautiful)!

- I am fearfully and wonderfully made!

- I am anointed of God for ministry. Hallelujah! I

- am an intercessor!

- I am a teacher of the Word! I

- am an overcomer!

- Thank you, Almighty God, for loving me, choosing me, and accepting me!

- Thank you, Lord, for being my vindicator, and thank you for fighting for me!

- I am reaping a 100-fold harvest from the seeds I sow into your kingdom Lord!

- Wealth and riches are in my house!

- All my household is blessed in their deeds. We're blessed when we come in and when we go out!

- I am wealthy and prosperous!

- I have abundance and no lack!

- I'm out of debt!

- Let God be magnified, He takes pleasure in prospering me!

- Money cometh unto me from the north, the south, the east and the west!

- I'll never be broke another day in my life! I

- have the blessing of Abraham on my life!

- The blessings of God are chasing me down and overtaking me! I

- am covered with blessings from head to foot!

- You have covered me with your favor today!

- I declare that you bless my coming in and my going out!

- I prosper in everything I put my hand to. I have prosperity in all areas of my life – spiritually, financially, mentally, socially, and physically!

- I am a giver. It is more blessed to give than to receive. I love to give! I have plenty of money to give away all the time!

- All that I own is paid for. I owe no man anything except to love them in Christ!

- Goodness and mercy follow me!

- Whatever I set my hands to shall prosper!

- Thank you, God, for giving me preferential treatment and special advantages!

- Supernatural doors are opening for me!

- I thank you God that you cause me to be in the right place at the right time!

- Thank you, God, for giving me the breaks and the promotions! The

- favor of God changes policies, rules, and regulations for me! People

- want to go out of their way to help me!

- No weapon formed against me shall prosper and every tongue that rises against me in judgment I am condemning!

  In Jesus' name, Amen!

ABOUT
BISHOP JOEL BROWN

Bishop Joel Brown, a third-generation pastor, was unfortunately not initially interested in following the call of God on his life. He pursued music (saxophone performance) and then law; practicing for several years in the Tampa Bay, Florida area. After having a vision from the Lord, during a particularly dark time in his life, Bishop Brown rededicated himself to the things of God and began pursuing God with all his heart. Bishop Brown is married to the lovely and gifted Tiffanie Brown and they are the parents of three handsome and brilliant sons; Joseph Wesley Brown, III, Joshua Wesley Brown, and Jonathan Wesley Brown. Bishop Brown is the Senior Pastor of Faith Celebration Church (Lakeland, FL) and he serves the North American Outreach Fellowship as a Bishop. Bishop Brown is passionate about Christ and he is devoted to building, training and equipping God's people (Eph. 4:11-16). Bishop Brown's passion is for the people of God to carry out the work of God's mission in their lives, their families, their churches and in their communities. In his free time, Bishop Brown enjoys eating good food with family and friends and playing the saxophone. Currently, Bishop Brown is pursuing his Doctorate of Ministry from Southeastern University.

Made in United States
Orlando, FL
22 June 2023

34433879R00024